Nostradamus Foresees Donald Trump, World War III and the Antichrist

Nostradamus Foresees Donald Trump, World War III and the Antichrist

Dylan Clearfield

G. Stempien Publishing Company

CONTENTS

1

Nostradamus Foresees Donald Trump, World War III and the Antichrist
Prophecies About the Modern Age

Dylan Clearfield

ISBN 978-0-930472-64-1
Copyright 2022 © by Prism Thomas
G. Stempien Publishing Company
Holy Island, Wales (editorial)

CONTENTS

INTRODUCTION

This book is about the predictions made by Nostradamus in his well known collection of quatrains, which are collected in segments known as the Centuries. The verses are called quatrains because the stanzas comprise 4 lines each. Not all of the verses in each quatrain have to be related, some refer to unassociated occurrences.

Nostradamus wrote mostly about European events that were to occur in his near future. As such, his works were quite popular with his contemporaries like the many astrological almanacs then in vogue. The people of his time were amazed at the accuracy of his predictions.

But some of his quatrains were either meaningless or gibberish, even when seen in the view of possible future interpretations. This accounted for a very small percentage of the whole. This can be attributed most likely to an unclear transmission of information from his spiritual source. Sometimes Nostradamus probably found it very difficult to literally hear what was being spoken or otherwise verbally related to him. This is common in spiritually transmitted knowledge.

Interpretations of the predictions are a matter of personal observation in all instances based on the best evidence available to the translator. Some people have access to more information than others. And, as in the case of this work, certain predictions could not be deciphered until the occurrence of specific events in the future. Until these specific events took place, the predictions did not make much sense. Now they do.

Many people have one major flaw in their interpretation of the quatrains of Nostradamus: they describe many of them as descriptions of historical events that had already happened before Nostradamus's era. That would make Nostradamus a simple historian, not a gifted visionary. His quatrains should be seen as predictions of what is to come, not what has been.

He will speak of things and places that a person of the 16th century could not have any acquaintance with. For example, Nostradamus clearly mentions the city of New York and the weapons and effects of nuclear war. How could he know these things unless inspired?

Some predictions point so clearly to a particular person or a particular event in the future that they are difficult to decipher erroneously or get wrong. You will see what these are as we proceed.

The predictions were written in French and a number of various translations were used by this author to reach the final version that is used in this book, including his own translation. However, there is very little difference among the translations. The primary difference lies in the interpretations placed on the meanings of specific words used in the quatrains. The reader will be the final judge as to the exactness or correctness of the interpretations found in this book.

NONE of the verses in the quatrains in this book were tailored to meet the predictions. In other words, all of the verses in this book come from translations made prior to 1600. Thus, in one prediction which is believed to be about Donald Trump, there is a group of words using the description of a *rigged election.* This was how the verse was written in the 16th century, long before Trump began making charges about rigged elections. The wording wasn't changed for a preconceived outcome.

The interpretations of the quatrains will be presented in a way that makes sense to the reader and which describes definite themes and are categorized by topic. Nostradamaus wrote hundreds of predictions in his book of prophecies - 100 quatrains per century (meaning number of verses in a section) - but they were mixed together and spanned different time frames. If a person wanted to follow a specific "story" that they told, the reader would have to select and arrange the quatrains himself. This task has already been performed in these pages.

The themes have been separated into 3 parts, with a 4th section devoted to a very interesting miscellaneous category, centering on a group of predictions of the future in which Nostradamus pinpointed with startling precision certain well known, major events of the 20th century.

Who Was Nostradamus?

Born on either the 14th or the 21st of December, 1503 in St. Remy, France, Nostradamus was baptized Michel, and he was one of at least 9 children. His grandfather Pierre had originally been Jewish but converted to Catholicism in about 1460 and Nostradamus followed the Catholic faith. He entered the University of Avignon at the age of 14 to study for his baccalaureate degree but had to leave after only a little more than a year's study due to the school being closed because of an outbreak of plague.

Nostradamus wandered the countryside for the next few years (1521 - 1529) studying wild herbs and preparing remedies from them for various illnesses. This led to his occupation as an apothecary and, most likely, this also led to his discovery of the methods for preparing what was later to be called the "rose pill." This was actually a lozenge upon which patients slowly sucked to extract the medicine which would cure them of the plague. By all accounts, this was something of a miracle remedy. Unfortunately, Nostradamus developed it too late to benefit his first wife and children who all died from an earlier plague outbreak.

In 1529 he'd entered the *University of Montpellier* to study for a doctorate in medicine from which he was soon expelled for supposedly "slandering doctors" by his effrontery of having once worked as an apothecary. After the deaths of his first wife and children in 1534 he traveled throughout Europe for more than a decade. He returned to France in 1545 to help battle another fierce outbreak of the plague in Marseille, using his "rose pill" lozenge to cure a great many people.

In 1547 Michel Nostradamus married a wealthy widow named Anne Ponsarde Gemelle and lived with her and the 6 children they had together in the town of Salon-de-Provence: three daughters and 3 sons.

One of the turning points in his life came in 1550 when he wrote his first almanac, almanacs being very popular items of the day. This is when he began to veer away from the practice of medicine to the study of the occult and astrology. His first almanac was so popular that nobility from all over Europe began to contact him for psychic advice and requested that he cast horoscopes for them. In conjunction with this, Nostradamus started writing predictions of the future and placed them in a book of 1000 quatrains.

So as not to draw the wrath of the Catholic Church, of which he remained a true adherent, Nostradamus wrote in coded verses but their meaning was still decipherable to those who sought to uncover the mystery. One of his most powerful admirers was Catherine de Medici, wife of King Henry II of France. Nostradamus was ultimately made counselor and physician-in-ordinary to the Medici's son who became King Charles IX of France.

Nostradamus lived between 1503 and 1566, reaching the age of 63. Most of his greatest works were written during the last 16 years of his life. He suffered from gout during his later years, a condition which worsened to the point that it made even simple movement very difficult. Finally, having a premonition of his nearing death, in late June of 1566 he called upon his lawyer and drew up a will which was generous to all members of his family.

Nostradamus was a 16th century personage. His vision, however, extended to the end of the world. But from where did his inspiration come? Outwardly he didn't appear to be overly interested in occult or mystical topics, aside from what he wrote in his almanacs. And even though he prepared horoscopes for clients he wasn't particularly involved with other practitioners of that art. It was as if he was compelled by a higher calling to write his predictions of future events.

We are fortunate in that Nostradamus described exactly the process he used to read the future. The secret was presented to the world in one of the first quatrains he wrote. That will be presented next.

CENTURY 1
1.11

The wand in the hand is placed in the middle of the tripod's Legs. He sprinkles with water both the hem of the garment and its (or his) foot. Fear, vapor and voice runs trembling through the robe's sleeve. Divine wonder; God sits nearby.

INTERPRETATION: Nostradamus, wearing a flowing robe, sits by a tripod which holds a bowl of water. He uses a wand to stir the water and also sprinkles some of the liquid onto his gown. He is at first fearful of the power he has contacted which arises with a vapor and shivers through the sleeves of his robe. Revelation strikes;

a spirit with knowledge of the future sits near him. And this is the manner by which Nostradamus received information from another realm about the future of this realm.

Later, there is another description of how his prophecies are given to him, speaking in the 3rd person.

CENTURY III
III.II

The divine word will give the substance, containing heaven and earth. Occult gold in the mystic act. Body and soul and spirit are all powerful. Everything is beneath his feet, as at the seat of heaven.

And then. At another location, in order to project himself from charges of using the black arts, Nostradamus wrote the following:

CENTURY VI
VI.C

May those who read this verse think upon it deeply. Let The profane and ignorant herd keep away. Let All astrologers, idiots and barbarians stay far off. He who does otherwise let him be priest to the rite.

Nostradamus obviously knew that he was writing dangerous material and was living in a time when this could cause him to be tortured or burned at the stake. After all, it seemed he could see the future. His own as well, which was proven for certain on the last day of his life.

And, finally, Nostradamus describes what will become of his body after his death in the next quatrain.

CENTURY II
II.XXVII

*The divine voice will be struck from heaven
and he will not be able to continue further. The
secret hidden until the revelation so that people
will walk both above and overhead.*

This quatrain tells us a great deal about himself. The divine voice that he'd been hearing will be struck from heaven means that he will die. The secret that will eventually be revealed will be his final burial place. After his death in 1556, Nostradamus was buried in an upright position according to his wishes between the great door and the altar of Saint Martha in a Franciscan monastery. This was so that no one would walk over his grave,

But during the French revolution his body was removed by soldiers and reburied in the ground in the Church of Saint Laurent.

So, it seems that Nostradamus knew about the events of his own afterlife as well.

Is Donald Trump the 3rd Antichrist?

Many people have speculated that Donald Trump might be the 3rd Antichrist. The belief that this might be true, however, is usually quickly dismissed when it is realized that his name does not add up to 666. While it is true that Donald contains 6 letters, John contains only 4 and Trump has only 5. However, what if his name is read in a different format?

Suppose his name was viewed as: Donald Johnny Drumpf? Johnny is just an extended version of John and Drumpf is his original family surname.

Donald is 6 letters. Johnny is 6 letters. And Drumpf is 6 letters. 666! Now he qualifies. But is he identified as the 3rd Antichrist by Nostradamus?

Why would Donald Trump be so important for Nostradamus to mention him as many times as he apparently does? Because Donald Trump may be the person who initiated the end of Democracy in the United States and brought in a fascist regime to be ruled by an autocratic leader (fuhrer). This isn't only a major event for the United States but for the whole world because of the collateral damage this would cause across the globe!

SECTION 1: Predictions about Donald Trump

Several of the quatrains of Nostradamus seemed to point directly at Donald Trump, family members and associates. As noted earlier, these exact verses of prediction were translated well before the modern era and as such were not tailored to fit a desired conclusion. The first quatrain seems to be specifically directed at Donald Trump and was written in the 16th century; but its true meaning could not be understood until the current era.

CENTURY VIII
VIII.XX

The false message about the rigged
election to run through the city, canceling the broken
pact. Voices bought, a chapel stained with blood,
the empire contracted to another one.

INTERPRETATION: *The false message about the rigged election to run through the city.* The first sentence is self explanatory - the complaint about a rigged election was a false message that was broadcast over a wide area.

Canceling the broken pact. The pact that was broken might refer to the commonly accepted agreement among parties in the United States that all elections are fair and honest.

Voices bought, a chapel stained with blood. Voices bought almost certainly describes commentators on television or on social media whose false message had been paid for distribution. A chapel stained with blood harkens to the damaged church outside of which Donald Trump stood holding a bible upside down while engaged in a "photo op."

The empire contracted to another one. The empire spoken of could have many meanings but may likely be concerned with the news and broadcast industry.

It would be difficult to devise a quatrain that is more directly referring to the "big lie" of the rigged election, using the very words that Trump so often used.

CENTURY VIII
VIII.XVII

*Those well-heeled will suddenly be cast
down, the world will be troubled by 3 brothers.
their enemies seize the marine city. Hunger,
fire, blood plague; all evils doubled.*

INTERPRETATION: *The world will be troubled by 3 brothers.* This quatrain is more closely directed toward the 3 male children of Donald Trump: Donald jr, Eric and their younger sibling Barron. Although Barron might not be as prominent as the other 2, his very presence in the family and its business interests troubles the world.

Those well-heeled will suddenly be cast down. The well-heeled who are suddenly cast down seems to describe U.S. Republican senators and members of the House of Representatives who cower under Trump's control.

Their enemies seize the marine city. What is the marine city that their enemies seize? That would be Seattle, Washington and their enemies would be Black Lives Matter protesters. This is one of the cities to which Donald Trump dispatched special forces to quell the activity.

Hunger, fire, blood plague; all evils doubled. Hunger, fire and blood certainly arose during these protests. The evils being doubled? This probably refers to the agitation increased due to the insertion of the outside forces by the then president. All during the early days of the covid plague.

CENTURY VIII
VII.LXXX

> *The blood of innocents, widows and virgins.*
> *So many evils committed by the Great Red One.*
> *The sacred images plunged into the burning*
> *candle-wax, terrified by fear none will be seen to move.*

INTERPRETATION: *The blood of innocents, widows and virgins. So many evils committed by the Great Red One.* This vision clearly is directed at the cruelty that was enacted at the border with Mexico, a brutality meted out mostly to women and children seeking asylum who suffered greatly under the Great Red One's (Donald Trump) policy of incarceration and separation of family members.

The sacred images plunged into the burning candle-wax, terrified by fear none will be seen to move. The sacred images refer to the holy candles that are commonly used by pious Mexican families and usually have likenesses of saints or Jesus or Mary painted on the outside of the glass bottle in which the tapers are burning. The terror of their treatment by the Great Red One forced these prisoners into a paralysis of fear, including fear of fleeing. Again: The Great Red One is Donald Trump.

CENTURY X
X.LXXXII

With the knives will come cries, tears and weeping. Not fleeing, they will make a final assault around the parks. They will set up high platforms, the living pushed back and murdered.

INTERPRETATION: This quatrain described the attack on the U.S. Capitol by insurrectionists on January 6, 2021. *With the knives will come cries, tears and weeping.* The knives represent all manner of weaponry that was used and the cries, tears and weeping are the sounds of the mad mob which did battle with the greatly outnumbered Capitol Police.

Not fleeing, they will make a final assault around the parks. The final assault will be around the parks, particularly Lafayette Park which was near the Capitol.

They will set up high platforms, the living pushed back and murdered. The platforms spoken of were set up all around the capital

complex as construction was ongoing at that time and were ultimately used as high places from which insurrectionists attacked as
well as being a good location on which to set up the scaffold to hang
Mike Pence. Anyone who watched the assault that day saw how the
police were steadily being pushed back with 5 of them dying later
from their injuries.

While almost all of the quatrains of Nostradamus have similar
translations made from the original French, this particular one has a
number of very different translations based on the same verses. This
of course leads to different interpretations of their meaning.

One interpretation that was made from an erroneous translation
suggested that this quatrain referred to King Harold of England
putting up a gallant last fight against the attacking Normans at
Hastings in 1066. But why would Nostradamus write a prediction
about an event that occurred about 500 years previously? That is
hardly a prophecy!

The primary problem with all the other translations is that they
include the word "instantly" in the last line as the translation of the
French word prinfault. *They will set up high platforms, the Living
pushed back and* (instantly - prinfault) *murdered.* I omitted the word
instantly from my translation because, according to all linguistic
research the word prinfault does not mean instantly. In fact, there
seems to be no such word at all. I believe that if it does appear in the
original version written by Nostradamus it was either an accidental
inclusion or as a meaningless word meant to confuse.

CENTURY X
X.XC

A hundred times the inhuman tyrant will die,
and a wise and caring man put in his place.
He will have the whole senate in his hands, he
will be troubled by a wretched scoundrel.

INTERPRETATION: *A hundred times the inhuman tyrant will die.* The tyrant referred to is Donald Trump. Like all hateful and paranoid individuals they seem to die with each threat or imagined threat.

A wise and caring man was put in his place. Trump was replaced by a wise and caring person - Joseph Biden. But the remainder of the quatrain still pertains to Trump.

He will have the whole senate in his hands, he will be troubled by a wretched scoundrel. Trump did have the entire senate under his complete command even after his loss of the presidential election, although the identity of the wretched scoundrel who troubled him can't be pinpointed because this was a role that could be filled by many.

CENTURY X
X.X

*Stained with murder and enormous
adulteries, great enemy of all mankind
he will be worse than his ancestors, uncles and
fathers. In steel, fire and water, bloody and inhuman.*

INTERPRETATION: *Stained with murder and enormous
adulteries, great enemy of all mankind.* Depending on your view of
Donald Trump, many people consider him a great enemy of all mankind. The enormous adulteries cannot be denied and he is stained
with many murders perpetrated in his cause.

He will be worse than his ancestors, uncles and fathers. Trump is
clearly worse than his father and those who came before him.

In steel, fire and water, bloody and inhuman. Steel, fire and water
point toward chemical and manufacturing industries of which his
rule as a businessman has been bloody and inhuman. A close fit for
Donald Trump? What do you think?

CENTURY II
II.X

*Everything will soon be set in order; we foresee
a very evil century. The state of the masked
and solitary people will be greatly changed.*

Few will remain to retain their ranks.

INTERPRETATION: *Everything will soon be set in order; we foresee a very evil century.* Everything will soon be set in order by the New World Order perhaps? It seems clear that we are facing a very evil century.

The state of the masked and solitary people will be greatly changed. The masked people must mean those who masked up for the long covid pandemic and many were kept in solitary confinement of one form or another to prevent infection. The reference to masked people clearly points to the Trump era (first term).

Few will remain to retain their ranks. During Donlad Trump's first term a great many of his appointees and employees at the white House resigned, not wishing to retain their rank working within the government. This ties the prophecy squarely to Donald Trump.

CENTURY II
II.XI

The younger son will succeed the elder very greatly. Raised to a kingdom of privilege. His harsh glory will be feared by all, but his children will be thrown out of the kingdom.

INTERPRETATION: This quatrain refers to the sons of Donald Trump rather than him directly. *The younger son will succeed the elder very greatly. Raised to a kingdom of privilege.* Eric Trump,

the younger of he and Donald Trump jr., is prophesied to become
even more powerful than his brother when it comes his turn to rule.
This of course implies a Trump dynasty.

His harsh glory will be feared by all. He will be a cruel ruler
and admired by some for his ferocity. For some reason his children
will be exiled from the kingdom - America under a dictatorship -
possibly for fear of their plotting against their father.

Much liberty was taken in interpreting this quatrain because the
French words had such a variety of potential meaning. But it does
seem a viable interpretation as presented because it fits well with a
possible future if Donald Trump senior does resume control of the
country.

CENTURY II
II.LXXXVII

> *Later a German prince will come from a distant*
> *country to a golden throne. Servitude is accepted*
> *from over the seas. The Lady subordinated in*
> *her time no longer adored.*

INTERPRETATION: This quatrain refers directly to Donald
Trump and his Republican Party. *Later a German prince will come
from a distant country to a golden throne.* The golden throne has
a very special meaning in this case. Most people know that Trump
has golden commodes installed for his backside pleasure and, of
course, throne is a slang Americanism for commode. His Germanic

background is factual, the original spelling of the family name being Drumpf. While he may or may not have come from royalty, Donald Trump acts as if he did and is treated as much by millions. So in a sense he came from a distant country (Germany?) to sit on his golden throne here.

Servitude is accepted from over the seas. The servitude that he accepted from overseas was that which Trump gave to Putin, dictator of Russia. Their relationship is well known and undeniable with Trump clearly the subservient. Didn't he plead for the help of the Russians to find Hillary Clinton's so-called missing emails prior to the 2016 election?

The Lady subordinated in her time no longer adored. The lady that has been subordinated is the Statue of Liberty. Trump and his allies desecrated the meaning of the message at the base of the statue, deriding the idea that we would accept the poor and helpless replacing it with the concept that America only welcomed the strong, powerful and white of color to its shores Nostradamus seems to have visited here in person to gather these facts for this quatrain.

CENTURY IV
IV.LVI

After the victory of the rabid tongue, the
spirit is tempted by tranquility and rest. Throughout
the battle the bloody victor makes speeches, enough to
roast the tongue, the flesh and bones.

INTERPRETATION: After the 2016 victory by Trump - the rabid tongue - he was tempted to take a rest, probably golfing somewhere. But he continued with his rambling speeches at his wild rallies.

CENTURY V
V.LXV

*On his sudden arrival, the terror will be
great, some of the ringleaders of the situation stay
hidden. The fiery lady will no longer be seen.
Thus, gradually, the lords will become angry.*

INTERPRETATION: This quatrain again refers to the insurrectionist attack on the capital complex on January 6, 2021. After all, the fall of democracy in America would be a major event for Nostradamus to record. *On his sudden arrival, the terror will be Great.* Donald Trump did appear at the outset to lead the march to the Capitol, one which he didn't make.

Some of the ringleaders of the situation stay hidden. Indeed the many people who arranged for and were behind the attack did stay out of sight and in the background.

The fiery lady will no longer be seen. The fiery lady would be the then powerful Speaker of the House, Nancy Pelosi who many of the invaders sought out but couldn't find.

Thus, gradually, the lords will become angry. The lords probably meant the various leaders of the government who were either under attack or were viewing it on television.

CENTURY I
I.LIII

Alas, we shall see a great nation
sorely troubled and the holy law in utter ruin.
All Christianity taken over by other laws, when
a new source of gold and money is discovered.

INTERPRETATION: This is a different type of quatrain which concerns the sociological effects of possibly Donald Trump and his followers. *Alas, we shall see a great nation sorely troubled and the holy law in utter ruin.* The troubled nation is the United States and the holy law that is in utter ruin is the one taught by Jesus Christ. The holy law in question is the basic belief presented by Jesus: love thy neighbor; turn the other cheek. Follow the Golden Rule. These ideals were countermanded during the days of Trump. He and his followers preached a doctrine of ruthless strength, taking advantage of your neighbor before he could take advantage of you; the ends justify the means. The very soul of the word of Jesus was questioned and put under attack. He was too soft and forgiving. Trump was the REAL chosen one.

When a new source of gold and money is discovered. The derision of the true Christian ethic was occurring at a time when a new form of money was being developed, specifically known as bitcoin and other similar currencies.

CENTURY II
II.LVI

One whom neither plague or sword could kill,
will die on a hilltop, struck from the sky. The abbot
will die when he sees the people, ruined in the shipwreck,
trying to hold onto the reef.

INTERPRETATION: This verse seems to prophesy the death of Donald Trump. *One whom neither plague or sword could kill, will die on a hilltop, struck from the sky.* The plague that could not kill him was his bout with covid 19 and the swords that could not harm him refer to the many negative items written (pen, mighty sword) about him.

The hilltop describes the hill on which the capital complex stands where Trump will be visiting. Being struck from the sky implies a lightning bolt or something like that which is an image that Nostradamus uses for a gunshot. *The abbot will die when he sees the people, ruined in the shipwreck, trying to hold onto the reef.* It isn't clear who the abbot might be - perhaps the governor of Texas Greg Abbott - but the ruined, shipwrecked people would be those who belong to Trump's party, lost without their leader, they now clinging to the political reef for survival.

This concludes the Nostradamus quatrains that were about Donald Trump. While it cannot be verified that these all were actually about Donald Trump and his administration, it seems certain that a few of them were, by simply taking into account their unique wording. For example - the quatrain about the "rigged elections" used the ex-president's exact wording. Also, the verses about the golden throne clearly seem to be directed at Trump.

That Trump and his administration's importance to the future was significant appears certain by the number of prophecies they inspired.

SECTION 2: Predictions about the Antichrist

There are very many quatrains describing the Antichrist and most of them are clearly stated as such. It is obvious that Nostradamus was hoping to warn the world of the coming of this evil man and hopefully to prevent the atrocities that he foresaw for the future. But there will be more than one version of the Antichrist's rise and more than one person named. This is because the future is malleable, and change could happen. Nostradamus covered all the alternatives. Will any of them point to Donald Trump or another world figure of our era?

CENTURY II
II.XXIX

*The eastern man will come from his seat and
cross the Apennines to France. He will
cross through the sky, the seas and the snows
and he will strike everyone with his rod.*

INTERPRETATION: The specific words used by Nostradamus in this quatrain are critical. *The eastern man will come from his seat and cross the Apennines to France.* The East could be any place from Russia to China but in this case probably means China. This is because Nostradamus chose to use the phrase *will come from his seat.* Rulers in great Asiatic countries were often associated with opulent thrones or seats from which they ruled.

He will travel by air and cross the great mountains to attack France. *He will cross through the sky, the seas and the snows.*

Then: h*e will strike everyone with his rod.* The use of the word rod is very significant. The rod of iron is a type of symbolic imagery associated by Scripture with Armageddon and Judgment Day. This seems to be the type of rod being wielded by this eastern man.

CENTURY X
X.LXXI

The earth and the air will freeze. There will be so much water. When they meet together to venerate on Thursday what shall occur will never be so fair. From all 4 directions they shall come to worship him.

INTERPRETATION: *The earth and the air will freeze. There will be so much water.* This implies a world where the climate has greatly changed, maybe due to some astronomical catastrophe and much of the world will be flooded.

When they meet together to venerate on Thursday what shall occur will never be so fair. Apparently a new form of religion has arisen where they worship on Thursday unlike any other current belief system. It seems like the people are coming to venerate the religion built around an Antichrist who chose Thursday as his special day, perhaps just to be unlike the other religions.

From all 4 directions they shall come to worship him. He has
control of the whole world, from everywhere he draws his disciples.

A quatrain apparently describing an Antichrist of the future
who has arisen to take control during some form of natural meteo-
rological crisis that has altered the world's climate; making it colder
instead of warmer as most people now are predicting. Perhaps, a
nuclear winter has occurred after an atomic war as was the popular
theme in the 1970's and 1980's.

CENTURY II
II.LXII

> *Mabus will soon die and there will happen a*
> *dreadful destruction of people and animals. There will*
> *be sudden vengeance, hundred hands of blood will cause*
> *thirst and hunger when the comet passes.*

INTERPRETATION: Nostradamus gives us a name - Mabus.
*Mabus will soon die and there will happen a dreadful destruction of
people and animals.* But who is Mabus? He seems to be a precursor
to the Antichrist because he will die. And then there will be destruction. Maybe he was a son, daughter or close relative of the
Antichrist.

*There will be sudden vengeance, hundred hands of blood will cause
thirst and hunger when the comet passes.* The only way that this part
of the quatrain makes sense is that as an image of the bloodied
hands of soldiers or warriors wreaking a quick horrible vengeance
on those who harmed Mobus, leaving a starved, parched world. This

will happen during the passage of a comet, but which comet it will be is not identified. Possibly it could mean Halley's Comet, but its next passage will be in 2062, 40 years from the publication date of this work.

This is a powerful quatrain which can be an imminent prediction for only 40 years into the future.

CENTURY II
II.XLV

The heavens weep too much at the birth of Androgyn;
Human blood is spilt near heaven. It is too late
for the great nation to be revived because of the death;
the awaited help comes soon, yet too late.

INTERPRETATION: *The heavens weep too much at the birth of Androgyn.* This again seems to point to some form of climatic upheaval; an abnormal amount of rainfall accompanying the birth of a being named Androgyn. This could refer to the historical son of Minos, named Androgeos whose death was something of a riddle to be solved since there are numerous versions of how he was killed. But the point for this quatrain is that Androgyn was a power figure who was born during some type of unnatural rainfall. This could be during some future weather catastrophe of global proportions.

Human blood is spilt near heaven. Warring aircraft will fill the sky. The only question is what type of aircraft are these people flying. And, remember, Nostradamus was writing these things in the 16th century, well before the first manned, controlled mechanical flight by the Wright Brothers in 1903. This does seem a very futuristic prophecy, envisioning craft even beyond our current capabilities.

It is too late for the great nation to be revived because of the death. This could be applied to any great nation of the future which has sustained a massive amount of death due to some form of warfare, possibly and likely the United States. This could be Donald Trump's so-called revived great America.

The awaited help comes soon, yet too late. This looks like a case where reinforcements of some type were anticipated but by the time they arrived they were too late to be of any help.

The cause of all the death and destruction was the person named Androgyn, born apparently during a period of climatic upheaval, as was the case with other Antichrists and their predecessors of the future. It appears we are being warned of the consequences that may befall severe climate change caused by unknown forces.

CENTURY II
II.XXX

A man is reborn from the infernal gods of Hannibal who will be the terror of mankind. Never more horror nor reports tell of worse things than will come to the Romans through babel.

A man is reborn from the infernal gods of Hannibal who will be the terror of mankind. The Antichrist is identified as coming from Northwestern Africa and from the location once occupied by Carthage, the home of Hannibal. Today, this location is the country of Tunisia. But it may go by a different identity in the future when the Antichrist arises

Never more horror nor reports tell of worse things than will come to the Romans through babel. Carthage - aside from Persia, later - was ancient Rome's most hated and persistent enemy. Three wars were fought between Rome and Carthage with Rome being victorious in all 3. After the final victory, the city of Carthage was leveled and sown over with salt so that nothing would ever again grow there. Nostradamus knew this and must've had a reason for wording the concluding portion of the verse as he did. Thus, babel represents news outlets of some form and the news that would've been utterly terrifying to Rome is that an Antichrist had arisen and he was from Carthage. So. if that was how Rome was supposed to feel, this implied that this new Antichrist would be, as the saying goes - "The world's worst nightmare." That was how the world would feel about his coming to power.

CENTURY VI
VI.XXXIII

*His forces made bloody by Alus, he will be
unable to protect himself by sea. Between 2 rivers he will
fear the military hand. The black and angry man will
make him repent it.*

INTERPRETATION: *His forces made bloody by Alus, he will be unable to protect himself by sea.* The name Alus is very important here. He seems to be engaged in a life or death battle for control of the world as might the Antichrist.

Between 2 rivers he will fear the military hand. The adversary of Alus is trapped between 2 rivers and appears to be on the verge of destruction. Unfortunately, he isn't named by Nostradamus.

The black and angry man will make him repent it. The black and angry man - yet unnamed - may be the Antichrist who will make Alus repent destroying the leader of the forces trapped between the 2 rivers. An ally of his? This sounds like a battle fought during the war of Armageddon or is one of the battles that preceded it. A difficult quatrain to decipher.

CENTURY VI
VI.LXXX

From Fez the kingdom will stretch out to those of Europe. The city blazes, the sword will slash. The great man of Turkey with a great troop by land so that the Persians will destroy the Christians.

INTERPRETATION: Once again, Nostradamus seems to be describing the preliminaries to Armageddon. *From Fez the kingdom will stretch out to those of Europe. The city blazes, the sword will slash.* The kingdom of Fez represents Morocco which will probably ally with Tunisia, another participant during the great wars. An unidentified city is destroyed by war and most likely represents all cities at this time.

The great man of Turkey with a great troop by land and so that the Persians will destroy the Christians. Among the mighty generals will be a personage from Turkey. He will be in charge of a massive Persian - Iranian - army which he will dispatch to eradicate all Christians in Europe.

Nostradamus is again outlining another scenario for the major battles and major participants of the war of Armageddon.

CENTURY VIII
VIII.LXXVII

The third Antichrist soon annihilates everything, 27 years
of blood his war will last. The unbelievers dead, captive,
exiled with blood, human bodies water and red
hail covering the earth.

INTERPRETATION: There seems little to leave to the imagination when interpreting this quatrain. After a 27 year war the Antichrist will have basically destroyed the world, leaving humankind in death and misery, pelted by a probably radioactive red colored hail of very unusual nature. The only real question: when will this happen?

This concludes the section where Nostradamus introduces his long list of possible Antichrists for a future that is always changeable.

SECTION 3: Predictions about World War III

Nostradamus made many predictions about the third world war. The reason they are differentiated here from predictions about the Antichrist is that these versions of the super great war do not propose the cause as being attributed to an Antichrist. They are the result of human animosities and end the way most wars do, warring nations using all of the weapons they have at their disposal. The results may be the same as if brought about by an Antichrist, but he is not a necessary component. Could Donald Trump be the catalyst who starts World War III?

There are many ways that our world might end, a naturally occurring World War III is one of them. And that is why Nostradamus has written so many varied versions of it. The future can always be changed; alternatives always exist.

Like the work of the brilliant quantum physicist Hugh Everett who decades ago assessed every possible scenario that would instigate a nuclear war, Nostradamus used his powers to envision all possible scenarios of nuclear war and those who might inaugurate it. He seems to have anticipated the great work of Hugh Everett the brilliant scientist who developed the doctrine of Mutual Assured Destruction (MAD).

CENTURY II
II.XLVI

*After great misery for mankind an even greater one
approaches, when the great cycle of the centuries is renewed;
it will rain blood, milk: famine, war and disease. In the sky will
be seen a fire dragging a trail of sparks.*

INTERPRETATION: *After great misery for mankind an even
greater one approaches.* With humanity having struggled through the
covid plague - and so many more before - it seems that this is the
great misery to which Nostradamus alludes here. But once we get
beyond covid - or the next pandemic - there will be something even
worse coming.

*When the great cycle of the centuries is renewed; it will rain blood,
milk: famine, war and disease.* Nostradamus was rather specific
about the timeframe here - shortly after the turn of the century disaster will occur. As of this writing, we're already 22 years into this new
century, so maybe the disaster will take place at the outset of 2200,
or beyond? Maybe a pandemic will strike the world again around
2218, like it did in 1918 and 2019! And then it will rain blood and
milk followed by famine and more disease. Indeed, Nostradamus
does repeatedly note how blood with rain upon us, probably of a
radioactive nature.

In the sky will be seen a fire dragging a trail of sparks. Many
people believe that this refers to a passing comet. I translate it as an

intercontinental ballistic missile bearing nuclear weapons. The trails
of sparks would be the flames pouring from the back of the missile.

CENTURY V
V.LXII

> *Blood will rain onto the rocks, sun in the east,*
> *saturn in the west, war near Orgon. A great*
> *great evil seen near Rome. Ships sunken*
> *and the tridental captured.*

INTERPRETATION: This quatrain seems very similar to the
one just examined. Here, blood will rain onto the rocks, probably
red and radioactive like in the previous verse. It will occur while the
sun is in the east - morning - and saturn in the west. This would
occur during an opposition of saturn. When this happens, saturn is
setting in the west while the sun is rising in the east.

*War near Orgon. A great great evil seen near Rome. Orgon could
be* a misspelling of Oregon or it could refer to the mountainous
areas of villages in alpine France. The great evil seen at Rome most
likely is the pope and the Vatican being savagely destroyed by the
Antichrist or simply being destroyed.

Ships sunken and the tridental captured. Ships would be sunken
during times of war but what is the tridental that is captured? It
could refer to the use of the tridentine liturgy of the Catholic Mass
- something Nostradamus would be very familiar with - being either
prohibited or bastardized by the Antichrist at this time.

CENTURY II
II.XXXII

Milk, blood, frogs will be prepared in
Dalmatia; battle engaged, plague near Balennes.
A great cry will go up throughout Slavonia; then a
monster will be born near Ravenna.

INTERPRETATION: Frogs will be added to the ingredients of nuclear fallout along with the blood and milk in this early battle of WWIII which takes place in Dalmatia(region on west coast of Italy). This is another possible scenario for the start of nuclear war.

Battle engaged, plague near Balennes. After the war begins, a plague suddenly breaks out in the area under attack. This is almost certainly a warning of the use of bacteriological weapons, which explains the final line: *a monster will be born near Ravenna.* The birth of a horribly mutated being.

CENTURY I
I.LXIV

*At night they will think they have seen the sun, when
they see a half-human pig man. Noises, screams, battle
fought in the skies. The dumb beasts will be
heard to speak.*

INTERPRETATION: *At night they will think they have seen the
sun.* This describes a nuclear explosion seen during the night, no
other bomb would have such intense brilliance.

When they see a half-human pig man. People who are experi-
encing this attack will see soldiers who are dressed in radiation gear
which have long snout-like tubes attached to oxygen canisters, thus
making them look like pig men.

*Noises, screams, battle fought in the skies. The dumb beasts will
be heard to speak.* A great deal of tumult will accompany this
battle fought with rockets and jets. And, when confronted, the half
human pigmen, which look like dumb beasts, will issue commands
probably through microphones which will distort their voices.

CENTURY I
I.LXXXVII

*Earthshaking fire from the center of the earth
will send earthquakes into New York City. Two great*

immovable powers will war for a long time, then
Arethusa the nymph will redden a new river.

INTERPRETATION: *Earthshaking fire from the center of the earth will send earthquakes into New York City.* Since volcanoes have not yet been reported to be brewing beneath the city of New York, this great fire is probably the result of a nuclear explosion at ground level, rather than a sky burst. Naturally, earthquakes will then shake the city apart. Remember, even though Nostradamus is writing in the 16th century he often refers to New York as the New City. This is the important identifier in this quatrain (as in many others).

Two great immovable powers will war for a long time. The United States and Russia. After the initial nuclear exchange, they continued fighting on various battlefields.

Then Arethusa the nymph will redden a new river. This line is quite difficult to make sense of. A guess would be that a new tactical weapon of the future called a nymph would be used to poison the waters of a river red.

CENTURY I
I.XCI

The gods will make it seem to mankind
that they are authors of a great war. Before, the sky was
seen to be calm, but now weapons will be used; the greatest
damage will be affected toward the left side.

INTERPRETATION: *The gods will make it seem to man-kind that they are authors of a great war.* Maybe this implies that some very severe natural disasters will occur simultaneously at this time which interrupts all communication across the planet, causing doubt as to if a war was being waged or not. A similar example would be the East Coast Power Failure of 1965 which, though not a natural disaster, knocked out communication leaving people in the dark as to if the loss of power was a natural event or was caused by a nuclear attack.

Before, the sky was seen to be calm, but now weapons will be used. Apparently, the previously mentioned natural disasters were not of the type in the upper atmosphere but were more like earthquakes, tsunamis and the like. But now, a war is being waged with rockets and airborne weapons possibly because one country thought it would be a good time to take advantage of another because of all the naturally caused destruction.

The greatest damage will be affected toward the left side. When looking at a globe, the United States would be on the left side, thus, this country would endure the most damage during this war.

CENTURY II
II.XCI

At sunrise a great fire will be seen, noise and
light extending toward the north. In the globe
death and screams are heard. Death awaits through
weapons, fire and famine.

INTERPRETATION: *At sunrise a great fire will be seen, noise and light extending toward the north.* There will be a nuclear explosion at sunrise and the devastation will spread northward. This implies some country in the northern hemisphere is the target.

In the globe Death and screams are heard. Death awaits through. Weapons, fire and famine. This is an unusually generalized quatrain by Nostradamus about world war III.

CENTURY VI
VI.XCVII

The sky will burn at 45 degrees, fire approaches
the new city. Immediately
a great flame leaps up when they want
to have proof of the Normans.

The sky will burn at 45 degrees, fire approaches the new city. Forty-five degrees is near the location of New York City on the map. The fire approaching the city is the initial burst that accompanies a nuclear detonation. Nostradamus seemed fully aware of this in the 16th century.

Immediately a great flame leaps up when they want to have proof of the Normans. This line does not appear to have any sensible interpretation. Maybe Nostradamus misheard the spirit voice that was speaking to him.

CENTURY V
V.XCVIII

*At the forty-eighth degree of the climacteric, the
end of Cancer, there will be a very great
drought. Fish in the sea, river and lake hectically
boiled. Bearne and Bigurre in distress from fire in the sky.*

INTERPRETATION: In this quatrain the location of the primary attack is at 48 degrees which can be Seattle or maybe Paris. *At the forty-eighth degree of the climacteric.*

At the End of Cancer, there will be a very great drought. The date would be about July 22nd when this drought will happen, but it doesn't seem like a naturally occurring one.

Fish in the sea, river and lake hectically boiled. Fish being boiled in unnaturally superheated waters is a recurring theme in Nostradamus's recounting of an atomic war in the future. *Bearne and Bigurre in distress from fire in the sky.* A fearsome airborne atomic explosion is the fire in the sky that superheated the waters in which the fish were boiled.

CENTURY II
II.III

Because of the heat like that of the sun on the

sea, the fish around Negreponte will be half cooked.
The local people will eat them
when there is a lack of food.

INTERPRETATION: *Because of the heat like that of the sun on the sea, the fish around Negreponte will be half cooked.* At first, this seems to obviously be a description of a nuclear blast causing the sea to boil. But, it is also possible that this refers to the Fukushima disaster of 2011 when the Japanese nuclear power plant almost exploded after being hit by a tsunami. Even though Nostradamus refers to the location being around Negrepont he may have confused it with a Japanese word he could not properly translate. Either way, this quatrain is about a nuclear disaster far in his future.

The local people will eat them when there is a lack of food. This did occur in the vicinity of the Fukushima disaster as well. The tsunami that caused the damage at Fukushima also devastated the surrounding region, leaving people homeless and without food to eat - except for the boiled fish in the irradiated sea.

CENTURY X
X.XLIX

The garden of the world near the New City, in
the road of the hollow mountains it will
be sieged and plunged into the tank, forced
to drink water poisoned with sulphur.

INTERPRETATION: *The garden of the world near the New
City.* This 16th century description could not be plainer: in New
Jersey (the garden spot of America) near the New city (New York)!!

*In the road of the hollow mountains it will be sieged and plunged
into the tank.* This too is shockingly accurate. In the area of the
United States just described there exists an underground shelter to
be used by government officials in the event of a nuclear war. What
will be sieged (seized) is some form of supplies being delivered to this
location after which a noxious element will be dumped into a tank,
probably a water tank. Why?

Forced to drink water poisoned with sulphur (British spelling).
What is being described is an act of internal sabotage. Someone
or some group attacks a supply truck or other delivery system and
replaces the contents with a poisonous element in order to kill
the people who had fled for shelter into an underground (hollow
mountain) facility during the onset of a nuclear war. This is how
Nostradamus envisioned the event in the 16th century.

This concludes the section on Nostradamus's predictions of
nuclear wars in the future. There are many scenarios for when and
where war might occur. It is wise to remember the final conclusion
of Hugh Everett in his study of nuclear warfare: in all cases the result
is MAD - Mutual Assured Destruction.

SECTION 4: Predicting Hitler, Hiroshima and Judgment Day

There's been some debate about whether or not Nostradamus actually meant to refer to Hitler and did really mean to point out the 2 cities of Hiroshima and Nagasaki in the quatrains about to be examined but, over the span of 4 centuries, his vision seemed be clearer than most of his detractors. Once again, his own choice of words provides proof of his visionary ability.

That being noted, we begin with one of his more confusing quatrains which some have suggested was meant to describe the near assassination of Adolf Hitler in 1939 by the same party led by von Stauffenberg which made a more well known assassination attempt in 1944 with the misplaced exploding briefcase.

CENTURY VI
VI.LI

The people gathered to see a new spectacle, princes and kings are among the onlookers. The pillars, walls, fall, but as if by a miracle the king and 30 of those present are saved.

EXPLANATION: Based on this verse, the well known astrologer named Ernst Krafft telegraphed Hitler to warn him that an assassination attempt would be made at a 1939 event he was attending to celebrate his beerhall putz made 16 years before. Hitler just finished making a speech at this event on November 8, 1939 and had left with several high ranking Nazis when a bomb hidden within a pillar detonated. Over 30 people were killed or injured, but Adolf and his staff escaped unharmed.

The reason that the verse is confusing is that neither Hitler nor his party was mentioned, and he was never known as a king. It seems that Nostradamus saw the event that was to transpire but only knew that powerful people would be targeted and escape harm.

Next to be examined are quatrains that more directly identify Hitler.

CENTURY II
II.XXIV

Beasts wild with hunger will cross the rivers,
the greater part of the battlefield will be won by Hister (Hitler).
He will drag the great one in a cage of iron
while the child of Germany rules without chains.

INTERPRETATION: *Beasts wild with hunger will cross the rivers.* This probably does not refer to living beasts like wolves and wild boar, or humans, but it probably is describing 2 forms of

German tanks used during World War II, the Panzer and the Tiger tank. These war weapons were voraciously hungry for fuel and were a fearsome sight when crossing rivers.

The greater part of the battlefield will be won by Hister (Hitler). One of the more controversial verses. Many authorities claim that the word Hister is describing a German river. But when taken in context with the other words in the sentence this makes no sense. How would a battlefield be won by a river called Hister? The word was meant to describe a human being and Hitler is clearly the most obvious candidate.

He will drag the great one in a cage of iron while the child of Germany rules without chains. The first part of this sentence must be symbolic, while the second half certainly describes Hitler as the child of Germany ruling without any constraint whatsoever.

Next is the final quatrain directly about Adolf Hitler and clearly is about this brutal, infamous leader.

CENTURY III
III.IIIV

*From the deepest part of Western Europe a child
will be born of a poor family, who will entice many
people with his speeches. His reputation will grow
even greater in the kingdom of the East.*

INTERPRETATION: *From the deepest part of Western Europe a child will be born of a poor family.* Adolf Hitler was born to a

relatively poor family in a small town in Austria which is certainly in
the deepest part of Western Europe.

Who will entice many people with his speeches. He controlled
many millions of people with his powerful oratory, a well known
fact. A prime example are his Nuremberg rallies where he spoke to
enormous crowds.

His reputation will grow even greater in the kingdom of the east.
Many authorities believe that the kingdom in the East being referred
to here is Japan. But much more likely the kingdom being referred
to in the East is Austria. The Austrian name for their country is
Osterreich which translated into English means the Eastern Kingdom. And, of course, this kingdom was forced to become part of the
German reich (kingdom) during the Anschluss of 1938.

The entire quatrain points directly to Adolf Hitler.

HIROSHIMA

CENTURY II
II.VI

Near the harbor and the 2 cities will
occur 2 scourges the like of which have never been seen.
hunger, plague within, people thrown out
by the sword will cry for help from the immortal God

EXPLANATION: *Near the harbor and the 2 cities will occur 2 scourges the like of which have never been seen.* The 2 cities were Hiroshima and Nagasaki, both of which were port cities and both which were destroyed by an atomic bomb blast that ended world war II. An event the likes of which had never before been seen, or even imagined. Yet, Nostradamus foresaw this in the 16th century.

Hunger, plague within, people thrown out by the sword will cry for help from the immortal God. These are the after effects of a nuclear attack with the only hope being to plea for help from the Almighty.

JUDGMENT DAY

CENTURY X
X.LXXIV

*The great 7000 years completed; it will
appear at the time of slaughter.
not far from the age of the great millennium when
the dead will come out of their graves.*

EXPLANATION: *The great 7000 years completed; it will appear
at the time of slaughter.* Nostradamus gives a timeframe, after 7000
years, but he doesn't specify from what point to calculate the begin-
ning of the 7000 years. It would seem that this would be calculated
backwards from the time of slaughter. This will probably be during
the nuclear war; count 7000 years backwards from then?

The second coming will appear at the time of slaughter to put an
end to it, as according to the words of the bible - the shortening of
these horrific days.

*Not far from the age of the great millennium when the dead will
come out of their graves.* Is the age of the great millennium 2000, 3000
A.D. or another time? Maybe the millennium starts when world
war III starts or at the second coming. A new age begins. Certainly
at the second coming it is prophesied that the dead will come out of
their graves.

There will be a day of judgment; Nostradamus has seen it.

HAUNTED HOUSE

CENTURY VII
VII.XLI

The bones of the feet and the hands were walled
up. Because of the haunting the house is uninhabited
for a long time. Digging in dreams the bones will be
unearthed, the house healthy and inhabited without noise.

EXPLANATION: Despite his Jewish heritage, Nostradamus was a pious Catholic. As such, he believed in ghosts, evil spirits and the rite of exorcism. In formal Catholic belief, ghosts are spirits allowed release from purgatory to perform penance on earth and hopefully to repair the damage of past misdeeds.

The bones of the feet and the hands were walled up. Because of the haunting, the house is uninhabited for a long time. At some point in the past portions of a person's body were placed inside of a wall. This caused the house to become haunted which kept it uninhabited for a long time.

Digging in dreams the bones will be unearthed, the house healthy and inhabited without noise. Due to a premonitory dream, the bones were removed from their place of concealment and were properly buried, which caused the house to be quiet again and fit for human habitation.

THE END

Lightning Source UK Ltd.
Milton Keynes UK
UKHW021258291022
411313UK00028B/766

9 780930 472641